GW00393551

PENNY TOOGOOD

Mindful

Contents

Foreword

I don't know about you but I feel most days that my my mind is constantly full of things. Things I need to do and things I need Andrew to do. Things that I'm worried about, things that might happen, things that might not happen, things that went well, things that didn't go so well. Everyday I have 1,000's of thoughts whirling through my head. Or sometimes it's just the same 2 or 3 thoughts that feel they are stuck on repeat.

There's times I feel like saying to my brain– "Will you give you head peace? Can I just switch you off?" I wonder where the button to stop this never ending cycle of thoughts that sometimes keep me awake at night. There's the "*I'm never going to be able to*," or the "*what if I can't?*" Even worse is looking back and over analsying everything you said and did which leaves you exhausted as you constantly come back to those two dreaded words " *if only..*"

We can often feel helpless at the mercy of all these thoughts. We even believe we have no control over what our minds do. Do you know want to know some good news? We do have control. We do have choice and we can stop the spiral of negative thoughts. We can get back in the driving seat and decide the direction of travel. Everyday we can make course corrections that keep us on the right track.

The world calls this being mindful. There are lots of helpful books that teach us to be in the moment - to be present. This means to stop being distracted by what might be and to focus and concentrate on where we are right now.

We can learn to stop catastrophising. This means allowing our minds to play out the worst case scenarios and we can learn to reign in those wild thoughts and get a reality check. We can fill our minds intentionally with good thoughts and be directive in our thinking.

So what do we think about?

We think about the fact that we matter. We think about the fact that we were created for a reason. We think about the fact that one much greater than us is holding the universe in His hands and is holding onto us everyday.

He's going before us and He's gone behind us. He's at our side. He never leaves us no matter how far we run and He never gives up on us no matter what we think or do. He's all in. When we allow our minds to be filled with these thoughts then we will find that love and life will flood our hearts and we will be at peace.

So come on a journey with me as we go through one of my favourite psalms line by line. Allow your thoughts to align with God's thoughts and to start to see things from His perspective as we read **Psalm 139** together. We will pause each day to reflect on what the Lord is saying to us and learn to hide His words in our hearts. As we discover these amazing truths our thinking will be transformed.

Let's be mindful of the fact that we are always on His mind.

Preface

¹ You have searched me, Lord,
  and you know me.
  ² You know when I sit and when I rise;
  you perceive my thoughts from afar.
  ³ You discern my going out and my lying down;
  you are familiar with all my ways.
  ⁴ Before a word is on my tongue
  you, Lord, know it completely.
  ⁵ You hem me in behind and before,
  and you lay your hand upon me.
  ⁶ Such knowledge is too wonderful for me,
  too lofty for me to attain.
  ⁷ Where can I go from your Spirit?
  Where can I flee from your presence?
  ⁸ If I go up to the heavens, you are there;
  if I make my bed in the depths, you are there.
  ⁹ If I rise on the wings of the dawn,
  if I settle on the far side of the sea,
  ¹⁰ even there your hand will guide me,
  your right hand will hold me fast.
  ¹¹ If I say, 'Surely the darkness will hide me
  and the light become night around me,'
  ¹² even the darkness will not be dark to you;
  the night will shine like the day,

for darkness is as light to you.

¹³ For you created my inmost being;
you knit me together in my mother's womb.

¹⁴ I praise you because I am fearfully and wonderfully made;
your works are wonderful,
I know that full well.

¹⁵ My frame was not hidden from you
when I was made in the secret place,
when I was woven together in the depths of the earth.

¹⁶ Your eyes saw my unformed body;
all the days ordained for me were written in your book
before one of them came to be.

¹⁷ How precious to me are your thoughts,[a] God!
How vast is the sum of them!

¹⁸ Were I to count them,
they would outnumber the grains of sand –
when I awake, I am still with you.

¹⁹ If only you, God, would slay the wicked!
Away from me, you who are bloodthirsty!

²⁰ They speak of you with evil intent;
your adversaries misuse your name.

²¹ Do I not hate those who hate you, Lord,
and abhor those who are in rebellion against you?

²² I have nothing but hatred for them;
I count them my enemies.

²³ Search me, God, and know my heart;
test me and know my anxious thoughts.

²⁴ See if there is any offensive way in me,
and lead me in the way everlasting.

Psalm 139

1

You have searched me, Lord

"**M**indfulness: *A mental state achieved by focusing one's aware-ness on the present moment, while calmly acknowledging and accepting one's feelings, thoughts and bodily sensations, used as a therapeutic technique.*" (Oxford dictionary definition)

There is so much talk today about mindfulness and the positive impact it can have on our mental health. I believe there is great benefit in being aware of our thoughts and feelings but when it comes to mindfulness the question I ask is mindful of what?

For many of us the problem is that our minds are full. They are packed to capacity with worries, niggling concerns, anxious thoughts and feelings of unease. Many of these thoughts are focused on external situations that we have no control over but for most people even when life is going well there can still be that underlying disquiet within. Our minds can be full of doubts and fears about who we are and who everyone else says we are.

We often prefer to keep a bit of distance between our true self and the self that we want everyone else to see. We like to have a polished version that doesn't make mistakes, fly off the handle or just can't be bothered at times. We think if people could see behind the mask they might not be happy with what they find, so we prefer to keep up the façade for fear that if people really looked closely they would be disappointed with what they discover.

So what is the answer? Do we simply acknowledge and accept these negative thoughts and emotions? If we focus on the present moment will that deal with our fear for the future or the guilt of the past. Do we simply try and empty our minds and not think at all? I don't know if you have ever tried to switch your brain off but in my experience it doesn't work. We might escape with trashy TV or a bottle of wine but we are only ever pressing pause.

If we want to find freedom in our thought life then we can't be empty heads. Instead we need to recognise that we can control what we fill our minds with. *"You will know the truth and the truth will set you free."* So what truth will free us? I believe it is the truth about what our Father in heaven thinks about us. Filling our minds with His words will bring calm in the storm and peace to our inmost being.

Many people feel afraid of even considering what God might think about them. Too many of us believe that our actions affect the way that God thinks and feels about us. So in order to maintain some sort of connection with God we try to keep us the facade. We are afraid of letting the mask slip because we are haunted by the thought " if God really knew what I was like, if He was to get inside my head then He would not be able to love and accept me."

God wrote poems for us. Words of life to fill our minds and hearts. Psalm

139 is one of my favourites. In this book I want to take you line by line, verse by verse and reveal to you God's heart of love for His children.

I want your mind to be filled with thoughts of His love, His goodness and His acceptance towards you. From the very first line I want you to discover that there is no need to live in fear. We are free to be ourselves, to be the person he created us to be. We don't have to hide or pretend. We can be real with Him.

Our father has *searched us.* Not with eyes of judgement but with eyes of love. He is not ignorant about our behaviour nor is He unaware of our imperfections. He has seen it all. He has observed very detail of who we are with a watchful gaze.

His response towards us is always love. He has no other framework to operate out of. He hates evil because it harms His children but He loves humanity and His response to all that He sees is to pour out His love. If we ever begin to doubt how strong this love is then we need to think about the lengths that He went to.

For God so loved the world, that he gave His only Son, that whoever believes in Him should not perish but have eternal life. John 3: 16

He gave His *only son.*

His posture towards us is always proactive. He doesn't wait to see how we fare, He is always moving in our direction. Whatever place we are in, whether we are seeking Him or are choosing to go our own way, He has made His position clear to us.

Jesus came to pay the price for our mistakes. He has made a way for us to receive God's love irrespective of our performance. When we put our faith in what Jesus has done for us at the cross then we can live life as our true selves. We don't hide the imperfections rather we allow the perfect one to clothe us with His love.

2

And you know me

How well do you know anyone?

It's a thought provoking question. We all acknowledge that relationships can be conducted on different levels. There's the people who live down the street from us. They have a dog and a young toddler and we say "hello" to them when we drop the kids off to school in the morning. We don't know their name but we smile and exchange pleasantries.

Next there's the people who we work alongside. They know a lot more about us, probably where we live and what our families are like. They might know what our hobbies are and the things we're good at. We may confide in them when we're having a bad day.

Then we have our close friends and family. The ones who know that when you say you're fine that there's something about your voice that is telling a different story. The ones who you let your guard down with and who sometimes get the wrong side of your tongue.

They are the ones you have dared to trust. The ones who have been allowed to see your weaknesses and vulnerabilities. Where you have felt safe enough to reveal the parts of you that don't go on show to others.

Finally we have our relationship with God himself. The one who made us. The one who has been with us everyday of our lives . The one who's with us 24/7.

Psalm 139 states that *"He has searched us and he knows us."* That means 100%. There is no area in our life that He has overlooked or has forgotten about. Every detail about what has made us who we are today is known by God. From even before we were conceived we were already part of God's plan.

Jeremiah 1: 5 tells us *"Before I formed you in the womb I knew you, before you were born I set you apart"*

God was there at the very beginning. He understands your journey. He sees what you have overcome. He has walked beside you through the ups and downs. There may have been times when you have wondered where He has been or if he was real at all. You might have spent a lot of your life doing things your own way. But that makes no difference to the Lord. He is committed to your well being not because you deserve it or have pleased Him but because he is a loving and gracious Father who is devoted to His family.

The Lord wants us to have an intimate revelation of the depth of His love for us. He has made us with a deep longing in our hearts is to be truly understood and accepted. He understands that we are afraid to be known in case we frighten people away. Sometimes we even feel afraid that God will turn away when He sees us warts and all. If he knows us completely could he still love us?

Remember back in the garden of Eden, when Adam & Eve sinned the shame overwhelmed them because they believed that once God knew what they had done He would no longer be pleased with them and they would be rejected. They were suddenly aware of their nakedness and they hid from God. If you know the story you'll recall that the Lord came looking for them. In that moment there were consequences for their choices but they were not abandoned or rejected by God.

Today we live in the finished work of the cross where all our sin has been dealt with. Past, present and future. We no longer need to fear our secrets being made known because the price for our wrong has been paid. We just need to believe in the saving work of Jesus.

How liberating to know that nothing can or will be hidden from the Lord. He doesn't want you to live in fear. He wants you to live everyday with the peace and assurance that He is leading you and He wants you to love getting to know Him more.

3

You know when I sit and when I rise

A re you someone who tracks how many steps you walk each day? It's something that has become part of many people's daily routines. It's always interesting at the end of the day to see if you have reached your target number.

Often I'm surprised by how many or few I have achieved. Many days can fly by and when we come to place our heads on the pillow at night the day's events can feel like a bit of a blur.

Today's verse shows us that no matter how preoccupied with the various daily tasks we get there is one who is mindful of it all. Each moment of the day our heavenly Father is tracking with us. Watching all that we do with interest, care and devotion. Every time we stop to rest He is there with us. Every time we jump up to tackle something new or merely push through the daily grind He is right by our side.

I feel that I would like to be more cognisant of this. To take those opportunities when I do get a moment to cease from activity and business, to check in with the one who is always attentive towards me.

We often tell ourselves *"but I just don't get a minute during the day"* and yet research would show us something different. Every minute of the day 1.4 million people are scrolling Facebook, 2 million people are searching on Tinder. On top of that 69 million Whatsapp messages are sent as well as 22.1 million texts, and 3.4 million Snaps are created. Not to mention the amount of viewers on YouTube, Netflix, and other social media platforms.

I don't say this to condemn anyone but rather to highlight the fact that as people who are often busy there is still a discontent that we can't resolve. An itch we can't scratch. We are searching and we are looking to find something that will satisfy the longing we have in our hearts. The desire to connect, to be known and to find fulfilment. I am challenged by the fact that when I feel restless inside, or when I have those spare few minutes, do I fill my head with endless information to curb the boredom or do I fill my heart with the eternal revelation of the Father's love and care for me?

The Lord knows me at all times. He's there when I sit and my thoughts wonder. He's whispering words of life and hope towards me but I often allow the noise of life and distractions to drown Him out.

Other times I convince myself that the day is too demanding for me to be able to commune with the Lord. I have somehow reduced my relationship with God to a short quiet time at the start of the day and then proceeded to fly solo from that moment on. This was never the way that God designed our lives. He never intended to sit on the sidelines while we got on with the important business of the day. He is more concerned about the things we are facing than we are. Deuteronomy 28:8 tells us *"You will be blessed when you come in and blessed when you go out."* The Lord wants us to approach our daily lives with the confidence that His favour is on us. We don't have to struggle with problems relying on our own wisdom and self effort. The Lord has given us His Holy Spirit who will lead us and guide us. He wants us to lean into His grace, to acknowledge Him and to know that when it seems like there is a roadblock ahead thatHe will make a way.

God sees everything that you face each day. He wants that to be a comforting thought for you. He not only sees it but He wants to be involved in your life. As you read these words today He wants you to be reminded of the fact that you matter to Him. He's inviting you to connect with Him, to listen to His voice, to allow His peace to flood your heart and mind giving you divine inspiration for every challenge that you face.

4

You perceive my thoughts from afar

What are you thinking?

This is a question I often ask my husband as I find Him daydreaming or looking very thoughtful as we drive along in the car. What I have discovered though is that sometimes I can be a bit disappointed by His answers. I often imagine he is thinking about us going away for a lovely holiday together or is pondering about what the Lord is saying for our family. The response is usually something to do with rugby scores, a new car or some comment by a politician that has annoyed him!

We regularly have a laugh at our expectations and how far removed they can be from the real life version of each other. In fairness my husband chooses not to ask me what I am thinking because it normally involves me organising every minute of His day with things that need to be done or things that I think would be helpful for Him to do. Maybe it's a male/ female thing or maybe I'm just a control freak and he is easily distracted, but we often struggle to really understand each other even when we have been together for such a long time.

Although we can at times think so differently we make sure every week to spend time together to connect and share our thoughts. We put aside the lists, we switch off from politics and we check in with how we are doing. What are you thinking about? What is troubling you? Do you feel filled with hope? Are you walking with a sense of peace? Do you feel assured that you are heading in the right direction?

We have learned that we can not be the answer to each other's problems or dilemmas but we can point each other to the one who can. When we take the time to hear each other, and allow the other person to be vulnerable and share what is on their heart we find that we can make sense of what we are feeling. We recognise that if we can feel love and compassion for each other, how much more is the Lord cognisant of the things that concern or occupy us.

David wrote many of the psalms and lots of them depict the incredible splendour of the Lord and how mighty He is. Psalm 8 starts with this amazing exaltation

"O LORD, our Lord,
   how majestic is your name in all the earth!
   You have set your glory
   above the heavens.....v 1

When I consider your heavens,
   the work of your fingers,
   the moon and the stars,
   which you have set in place,
   what is man that you are mindful of Him,
   the son of man that you care for Him? v 3-4

This is our awesome God, the creator of the universe, the one who is supreme over all. And now David reminds us in Psalm 139 that the one who reigns in heaven is interested in us. He perceives everything that is going on in our lives. Our thoughts that can be one moment so fleeting do not escape the Lord. Our deep meditations that expose the very core of who we are, are laid bare before our heavenly Father. So often in life we choose to hide our true thoughts because we are afraid of looking stupid or fear that letting people in on what's actually going on will lead to them thinking less of us. But with the Lord we do not need to fear. He knows us and He understands us. What's more He is committed to our best. He does not judge us, or reject us because our thinking strays away from what He would will for us, but he lovingly reminds us of who He has made us to be.

As we read in Psalm 100:3

Know that the LORD, he is God! It is he who made us, and we are His; we are His people, and the sheep of His pasture

5

You discern my going out and my lying down

A re you someone who is very aware of their physical surroundings and could explain in detail the specific route to get to places? I wish I was more like that. I can be driven from one place to another and realise that when you I get out of the car that I have absolutely no idea how I got there. I struggle in the whole area of navigation and I have to really lean in and concentrate if I am travelling somewhere for the first time. If i don't then I am fairly certain that I won't be able to find my way home again.

For a number of years this was an area in which I really experienced fear. It would limit me from going to particular places as I worried about getting lost. I wrestled with these negative emotions and felt very frustrated with myself. I often encouraged others to step out and trust God in many situations and then with something that seemed so simple like driving I was admitting defeat and missing out on opportunities. I recognised that I had to come to a place where I began to take seriously all the verses in the Bible. I knew that the Lord was with me at all times no matter where I was and yet it was not making a difference when it came to my behaviour or the choices I was making. For some reason I could not accept that the Lord being with me meant that He would help me. He wouldn't stand by and watch me struggle but it actually meant He was interested in my well being and was invested in taking care of me.

We all battle with different things. For you driving might not be a problem but if you are asked to give a presentation at work, or told that you have to phone someone that you have never met before you might want to run in the other direction. There are things that we don't feel qualified for. Tasks which push us way out of our comfort zone and we worry that if we step out of the boat we are not just going to fall into the water but we are going to end up drowning!

At moments like these I have learned to meditate on the fact that God is my Father. He is not observing from a distance but He is paying close attention to every detail of my life. He looks with eyes that are committed to protecting me. He wants me to learn to trust Him, to give Him the things that are holding me back and to step with boldness into the life without limits that He has ordained for me. His favour is on my life. He has lifted me from the miry clay and set my feet upon a rock. Now I can stand with confidence that His Spirit will empower me to stretch beyond what I believe I am capable of and to reach out for new opportunities.

Moreover when I read today's verse I love the fact that nothing escapes His notice. He

"discerns my going out and my lying down."

Many people fall victim to oppressive thoughts that keep them awake at night. Increasing numbers of people, including Christians, find night time a struggle. The physical darkness can heighten the dark thoughts that plague our minds. Those things that can niggle us during the day can become magnified during the long, dark hours of the night. We can feel isolated and overwhelmed, confused and exhausted as we attempt to find some rest for our troubled minds.

The Lord wants us to know that He is there. Through the nights When we sleep like a baby and wake up ready to take on the world. The nights we have wrestled with fears and doubt and have barely slept a wink. He has watched over us and He has been right by our side. The heart of the Father is revealed in these verses in Philippians 4, v 6-7 that remind us where to turn every minute of the day, in every situation.

Do not be anxious about anything, but in every situation, by prayer and petition, with thanksgiving, present your requests to God. And the peace of God, which transcends all understanding, will guard your hearts and your minds in Christ Jesus.

Remind yourself today that not only is the Lord with you, He is there to lead you, to guide you, to protect you and to pour out His love and acceptance towards you.

6

You are familiar with all my ways

D o you ever have those moments when you think to yourself I really hope no one was looking? There are times when we feel like we have made a fool of ourselves because we trip and fall flat on our faces. What was it for you? Getting your coat caught in the door, treading in dog muck, or leaving the house wearing odd socks or even worse, odd shoes?

There is such pressure in today's world to present an image of being perfect. The perception is that there is a low tolerance for people messing things up and making mistakes. So we all try to hide the imperfect parts of ourselves in case people become disappointed with us. Living like this however becomes very tiring as we try to keep everything just right. And yet the one thing that brings us together and helps us connect with others is our vulnerability. We actually prefer it when people are real with us. They don't just show us the Facebook version of their lives where everyone is smiling and the kids are all happy. They show you the real version where the teenager doesn't want to be in the photo, the Dad gets annoyed and then the Mum gets frustrated because the nice family day out is ruined! We don't want to put that photo up, the kids taking

MINDFUL

lumps out of each other and Mum and Dad doing death stares!!

I remember a number of years ago going to a big Christian conference in London. The whole thing was so impressive from the moment we got off the train. There was a group of volunteers sent to the train station to greet you and show you the way. There were complimentary gifts given out at the door. The whole venue was decorated with such incredible style and the atmosphere was amazing.

But the one thing that stands out to me the most was the main speaker. I actually can't remember what her message was that day. I don't remember what she said but I remember how I felt. Sometimes at big events we can feel overwhelmed. Everything can look so impressive, so professional, so perfect. And yet when the lady got up to speak the first thing she said was. " Sorry about the shirt!"

At first I didn't know what she was talking about because we were sitting near the back but then it became clear as she began to explain. Apparently about 10 minutes earlier she had spilled a whole cup of coffee down her front.

Her immediate reaction was to panic and think "how on earth can I stand up in front of all these people with a huge coffee stain at the front of my clothes?! What will everyone think?" After deliberating for a couple of minutes if there would be time to change or if someone could swap their clothes she decided there was no need to fuss.

" What am I worrying about?" she said. "We're all family here!"

By stepping back for a minute she recognised that she was in the presence of thousands of people who loved Jesus. Why should she need to be concerned about how she looked. People were there for a much more

18

important reason anyway. She shifted her perspective and fixed her eyes on what was most important and in doing so I believe her authenticity broke the ground for people to receive her message.

Everyday we are faced with moments we would rather undo. Nothing will ever go quite according to our plans. Although when I think back at that conference I realise for me it helped me to see past the bright lights and platform and see a normal person like me and you. It's easy to think that life is so much easier for other people. They don't have the same struggles, the same challenges, the same insecurities. But that is not the case. We are all going through life with different types of stains on our tops from the various experiences and challenges we have had to walk through. The great thing about knowing the Lord is that there's no need to try and hide those things that we feel embarrass us or make us look weak. In fact the Bible tells us to rejoice in our weakness because when we are weak then He is strong.

I felt at ease when I was allowed to see someone else's imperfect day. God used what could have been seen as a negative to minister to a whole stadium full of people that we don't have to pretend. We can be real. We were made to be authentic and the parts of our lives that we feel embarrassed about are actually areas where His grace will shine through even stronger and bring life to those around us.

7

Before a word is on my tongue you, Lord, know it completely

This is something my husband and I find ourselves saying to each other more and more these days. It seems the longer you have lived with someone the more you get to know them and the more you start to be able to predict how they are going to react to different situations.

Andrew's constant mantra is " Did you switch the lights off?" whereas mine is " Did you put the bin out?" We get so familiar with each other's habits, our points of frustration or the things that make us laugh.

Meal time is another part of the day when you know you are going to hear certain positive or negative comments from various members of the family. Two members of the family out of 5 groan when it's chille for dinner. 1 out of 5 will not eat mashed potatoes and 3 out of five love avocados. I can anticipate the responses before I have even turned the oven on. We can all become so predictable.

And yet there are times when although we are so familiar with each other, we still struggle to really understand what might be going on in the internal worlds of those closest to us. We can share our hopes and dreams, our challenges and disappointments and yet sometimes we still fail to properly articulate all that we feel inside. There are times we grapple with the words that we use. It can feel like they are inadequate at really communicating all that we feel and think. We wrestle with our emotions and we find our thoughts confused or illogical and then we don't want to express our thoughts because we feel a pressure to have our lives together. We live with a sense of expectation that we should know what we think, where we are going and what we want to do. Then often because we feel like we don't have all our ducks in a row we leave some words unsaid. We think, *"they won't understand." "They will take it the wrong way," "they won't think of me in the same light."* And we retreat back behind the mask and say the words we think others want to hear from us rather than what we truly think deep down.

The great comfort for me is that the Lord knows it all. Before we utter any words. Those deep thoughts that we wrestle with and hold back from sharing- He knows them. He doesn't judge us or change how he feels about us, He simply loves us. Furthermore He is longing for us to bring those thoughts to Him. To let Him into those silent fears that are keeping us from being real with the people around us. He is wanting us to enter into a dialogue with Him where we let our guard down and say *" This is what I really think! You might say you will always be there for me but there are times I feel alone. You might say you are my healer but I am struggling with this sickness. You might say you are my provider but I can't pay the bills this month."* The Lord wants this brutal honesty because it is in this place where you expose what is really going on that He can begin to shine the light of His love and grace into your heart. he wants you to allow His faith to grow on the inside of you so that the things you currently see and experience will be consumed by the incredible force of His grace as it is released in your life.

Our inner world will always be the catalyst for change in our outer world. The situations, challenges and possibilities that lie before us will seem insurmountable until we recognise our true position as sons and daughters of the King of the universe. The words we speak have power and authority and the words that the Lord is whispering in our minds are words of victory, words of healing and words that establish His rule and reign over every part of our lives.

Psalm 97:5 tells us that " *The mountains melt like wax at the presence of the Lord*"

The Lord knows all the words that pass through your mind everyday. His word is infused with life giving power and overcoming might. When your words are full of defeat don't try to hide and turn away or pretend and put on a mask. Instead turn to Him and be real. Allow Him to lift those burdens from your shoulders and allow His words to ignite your heart and bring His heavenly reality into your world.

8

You hem me in behind and before

I was recently watching a travel programme about a man visiting Iceland. One of the things that he got to do on his adventure around the country was to see sharks up close. My first reaction was he must be absolutely crazy- how on earth can it be safe to get into the sea and be surrounded by sharks? I was intrigued and petrified at the thought of this and I could hardly bare to look as the programme unfolded and they showed how this was going to happen.

A special metal cage had been built that was lowered into the deep water from the side of the boat. The cage remained attached to the boat so it was like being lowered in a small prison cell amongst a large shiver of sharks. (That apparently is the correct group noun for sharks!) Then sharks came up close to the bars of the cage. They actually swam within inches of the guy but they could not harm Him as he was completely surrounded by the metal enclosure and no matter how sharp or strong the shark's teeth were they were not getting through.

I can't say that after seeing this I felt any more inclined to go underwater and see sharks up close, but it did make this verse come alive when I read it today. We live in a world where there is danger. We can feel like we are surrounded on every side. Often as believers we want the Lord to remove the danger from us so that we don't even have to be faced with difficult circumstances. But we need to remember that the Lord didn't promise a trouble free life. He actually said in this world you will have troubles. We shouldn't be surprised when we are faced with opposition or trials, but we should also not be overwhelmed by them because Jesus also told us in the same verse to "Take heart as he had overcome the world."

You might have been going through a trying situation and you have wondered whether you are going to make it through to the other side. I believe today the Lord is reminding you that no matter how close the danger may feel it will not harm you. You are *hemmed in*. The word is also used when a city is laid under siege. It means *You entrap me. You encircle me, behind and before. You will not leave me alone.*

The Lord is more committed to us than we can ever imagine. He is more invested in our well being and more concerned with seeing us reach our potential than our minds can begin to grasp. We will not avoid all adversity. In fact at times we will come face to face with the one that is out to destroy us. But His promise is that we will be delivered. We will walk through the valley of Baca and where we believe that we could be consumed by the enemy. we will walk out stronger. Every time that happens we will have a greater boldness and conviction of God's faithfulness.

When we are allowed to walk through hard times it is for our ultimate benefit. The Lord takes what the enemy was trying to use to defeat us and uses it as a stepping stone to bring us closer to the plans and purposes that he has laid out for us. Too often we can allow our small thinking to hinder what God can do in us so He needs to show us who we are in Him.

Only when we are faced with danger can we begin to fathom that we no longer have a spirit of fear but of power, love and of a sound mind.

When you pass through the waters, I will be with you; and when you pass through the rivers, they will not sweep over you. When you walk through the fire, you will not be burned; the flames will not set you ablaze. Isaiah 43:2

The Lord is surrounding you on every side. You may have to walk into the fire like Shadrach, Meshach, and Abednego, but remember what the king saw when they were inside it:

I see four men loose, walking in the midst of the fire, and they have no hurt; and the form of the fourth is like the Son of God. Daniel 3 : 25

and when they came out people were amazed

upon whose bodies the fire had no power, nor was a hair of their head singed, neither were their coats changed, nor the smell of fire had passed on them. Daniel 3 :27

When you come out of your trial the only thing that people will see will be the glory of the Lord on your life.

9

You lay your hand upon me

When Jesus walked the earth one of the things that marked Him out from the religious leaders was His interaction with everyday people. He was not distant and aloof like many of the priests and Rabbi's of the day. He did not judge and look down on people. In fact He did the opposite. He got down to their level. He spent time with them. He listened to their stories. He accepted them no matter what mess was in their lives. He responded with gentleness and compassion. He sought to understand where the people were but He didn't leave them there. He showed them a better way.

Think of the story of Zacheaus. While everyone else despised him and saw only a cheat and a thief, Jesus saw past the ugly parts of His life to a lost man who was looking for love and acceptance. He saw a man who had tried to fill the void in His life with all the wrong things. Jesus offered him the hand of friendship and loved him back to a place of wholeness. Zacheaus changed His behaviour not because he was made to feel bad about his choices, but because he experienced love that he didn't deserve and it unlocked a love within Him that he didn't know existed before.

Look at how Jesus treated the leper. The one who was excluded from society as he was a risk to others. His disease was not of the heart like Zacheuas but His disease was physical. Visible for all to see. He was an outcast because people were afraid. They didn't want to catch what he had. He had been banished to a life void of physical contact. But when Jesus sees him what does he do?

Jesus reached out His hand and touched the man. "I am willing," he said. "Be clean!" Immediately he was cleansed of His leprosy. Matthew 8 v3

Jesus not only healed the man but He restored his dignity. There were other healings when Jesus just spoke the word and the person was healed but Jesus knew this man not only needed His body to be made well but he needed to feel whole again. This man needed to know that he could receive touch from others. When Jesus reached out His hand He was showing the man that the invisible barrier that had been created keeping him isolated from society had been broken. He was freed from a cursed life and was now able to step into a new life of love and acceptance.

Look at how Jesus responds to Peter as he steps out in faith and walks on water. When the wind starts to rise all around him and the waves feel like they will overwhelm him, Jesus steps in. He reaches out His hand and rescues him. This story shows us that our fear will never be greater than His ability to save and deliver us.

The picture I love the most of the Lord's hand is when we see Him with the children. The disciples get carried away and make decisions above their pay grade about the Lord's capacity and energy levels. They think that they are doing Him a favour when they send the children away. Surely the Lord has more important business to attend to?
   I love His reaction.

People were bringing little children to Jesus for Him to place His hands on them, but the disciples rebuked them. When Jesus saw this, he was indignant. He said to them, "Let the little children come to me, and do not hinder them, for the kingdom of God belongs to such as these. Truly I tell you, anyone who will not receive the kingdom of God like a little child will never enter it." And He took the children in His arms, placed His hands on them and blessed them.

   Mark 10: 13-16

Jesus places His hands on them and blesses them. He shows them they are valuable, they are worthy and moreover His blessing is on their lives. They can expect to see favour and goodness because that is the Lord's heart for them.

   Today we can have such confidence because Psalm 139 tells us that he lays His hand on us. He bestows upon us every good and perfect gift. We can turn to Him for friendship, for healing, for deliverance and for favour.

'Because *the hand of the Lord my God was on me*, I took courage...' (Ezra 7:28).

God's hand is also on you: leading, guiding, encouraging, protecting, strengthening you and giving you courage. Let your mind be filled with the truth of His hand of blessing on your life.

10

Such knowledge is too wonderful for me. It is high, I cannot attain it

I 'm not sure if you are what you call a natural student or if you struggled through your school days. I was always very conscientious, what my husband would term a girly swot! But despite my best efforts to work hard and apply myself there was one subject that I just could not master no matter how much time I seemed to invest.

I think we all have natural tendencies towards different aspects of education. Some of us are musical, others love maths, languages or art. Then there are those that love science. Those who love to find out how things work and discover incredible insights about the world around them.

I, even though I loved nature and the beauty of creation, could not get my head around physics. It all felt too abstract to me. Forces that I can't see. Atoms that are too small to be perceived. Gravity and a dozen other topics. I used to feel like my brain ached when I came out of a physics lesson as it was all just too much to take in.

I used to believe that science was at odds with faith as theories such as evolution were presented as facts. You could be seen as being naive if you trusted in a creator rather than a scientific process. Now I realise that science is in a game of catch up as it attempts to make sense of the work of a higher being who is infinitely more vast than our minds can imagine. Even if every man were to devote a life time of study to search the mysteries of the earth they could never begin to fathom them.

Now I find I have a new interest in this world of science as I realise that every discovery, every new step forward actually just points back to the one who created it all. Science simply unveils the secrets of God's Kingdom. Science uncovers the magnitude of creation and our master creator. I now understand that at times my head did struggle to take it in because our thinking is limited. We are constantly being challenged to expand our thoughts past what we have experienced and what we know to be true and we are invited to go deeper and take a step of faith to trust that what we know is only in part.

Our God wants us to know Him, but this is a journey that begins in this world and will stretch into eternity. We will never exhaust our knowledge of how incredible He is. We will simply discover layer upon layer of riches and treasures. These treasures have been hidden from before the foundation of the earth. They have been kept secret so that as we search we uncover greater riches that point to His power, His precision and His attention to detail. Your Father in heaven cares for His creation, for His people, His family and His children.

The thing that brings me such joy is when I consider that the God of the whole universe, the one who holds it all together, who set the stars in the sky, who rolled back the sea, who can move mountains and raise the dead, has a personal interest in me. Not only did He choose me, but He is committed to me for the rest of my days. He sees me as significant. He has so much confidence in me that He has chosen to work out His plan of salvation to the world through me.

We are not meant to be able to figure it all out. But instead we are drawn in by the immeasurable complexities of our God. He wants us to marvel in the mystery. He wants us to be overwhelmed by the greatness of His power and then He wants us to realise that He did all of this for you and me. This knowledge is too much and that means we can't exhaust it. We can't fathom it and become bored or apathetic. When we search we will continue to discover and we will never be left disappointed.

11

Where can I go from your Spirit

Where can I flee from your presence?

"You can run but you can't hide." I remember this line in a Phil Collins Song. Many of us have probably been familiar at one time or another with the sentiment behind it. I know there have been moments in my life when troubles have overwhelmed me. Times when I have been overcome with fear and I have lost hope that things will ever be able to turn around. At moments like these when we cannot see a way forward our only desire is to escape. We dream about running away to start afresh. We picture ourselves in a new place where no one knows our past and where no one will judge us. A place where our mistakes are not surrounding us and circumstances can line up in our favour.

Have you ever stopped to think about what it is that is motivating you to want to flee in that moment?

I believe it is because we feel ashamed. When we feel shame we instinctively want to turn away from God. We know in our hearts that

God is good and just so when we act in a way that is contrary to His nature the word tells us that our hearts condemn us. This is the work of our conscience and not the work of the Holy Spirit. Many people have mistakenly believed that their conscience and the Holy Spirit are in effect the same thing. They have listened to that voice inside and determined that must be the Lord pointing out their faults and trying to get them to act better. However that is not the role of the Holy Spirit. Remember Jesus' words in John 14:26

But the Advocate, the Holy Spirit, whom the Father will send in My name, will teach you all things and will remind you of everything I have told you.

The Holy Spirit will only remind you about what Jesus says about you and why Jesus came

"*that whoever believes in Him shall not perish but have eternal life.*"

It doesn't say whoever behaves right, it says whoever believes.

Let's read the full verse in 1 John 3:20

"*Even if our hearts condemn us, God is greater than our hearts, and He knows all things.*"

Before we came to know Jesus we had a debt to pay for our sin, the devil could come and accuse us and we had no one to plead our case. But because Jesus came to redeem us, it means He bought us back and cancelled every debt. There is no longer an outstanding payment that you need to make and He is now our advocate. Even if your heart is telling you one thing you can speak to your heart and reassure it of your true standing now that you are in Christ.

This is made clear to us in the letter to the Hebrews:

"let us draw near with a sincere heart in full assurance of faith, having our hearts sprinkled to cleanse us from a guilty conscience and our bodies washed with pure water." Hebrews 10:22

Many of us feel that we need to flee from God because we are living with guilt and shame over our actions. We understand that we cannot flee from God because He is all knowing. Therefore our response is to withdraw from Him. Why is this? We turn away from the one who we believe will judge us. It's almost like when a child does something wrong and they know they are going to be found out. They close their eyes in the hope that if they can't see you then maybe you won't be able to see them!

In spiritual terms this is what we do with God. Often we are still believing the lie the enemy tells us that we can not approach a holy God with all our sin and mess. However most of us feel a torment inside as we know that "we cannot flee from His Spirit" Therefore in our shame we simply can't bear to look into the face of the one we believe we have disappointed.

This is where the second part of this verse becomes so significant, 'Where can I flee from your presence'' The word *presence* is' 'Mippaneycha'' in Hebrew which can also be translated 'from thy faces.' God's presence is His face, we cannot flee from it. In fact, now through Jesus we can come and look Him straight in the eye and know that He will not hide His face from us. He will not only invite us into His presence, but we can expect to receive His goodness.

Let us therefore come boldly unto the throne of grace, that we may obtain mercy, and find grace to help in time of need. Hebrew 4: 16.

What an incredible saviour we have!

12

If I go up to the heavens, you are there

if I make my bed in the depths, you are there.

I recently found myself getting frustrated with my daughter one afternoon after school. She was sitting trying to do her homework project on the Romans. She asked my advice on what to draw and after searching online for various examples we came up with a tutorial on YouTube on how to draw a Roman soldier. This seemed perfect as I am rather lacking in artistic talent so I felt at least I had found someone who could point her in the right direction! She happily sat down with a blank sheet of paper and set to like a young Picasso ready to produce a masterpiece.

After at least half an hour of stopping and starting the video and careful copying and rubbing out I was surprised to hear the sound of paper being scrunched up and promptly thrown on the floor. The laptop was slammed shut and she sat there with red eyes and a sad face.

What had seemed to be going so well had suddenly ended in complete disaster. " I can't do it!" "It's too hard! I can't draw!" I reached down to pick up the piece of paper and as I unravelled it I discovered a brilliant drawing and one of which I would have felt very proud to do. I tried to encourage my daughter that this was fantastic, but in her eyes it just wasn't good enough. The arms weren't right and apparently this meant the whole thing was ruined. "I just can't draw people!" she exclaimed.

I tried to console her and we talked about what else she could draw. We went back online looking for other more easy Roman stuff but after another half an hour of trying the Colosseum, Roman baths and Chariots I was starting to feel like we were descending into a black hole of artists block.

It wasn't Sophie's artistic talent that was the problem. It was the way she viewed herself. She had slipped into the mindset of "I can't do it" which was quickly followed by the lies of "I'm no good." As she started to believe this her confidence began to evaporate and she began to lose her sense of value. Suddenly not being able to draw a Roman soldier on a first attempt was equal to not being a very worthwhile person.

This may seem a bit dramatic, but if we are honest how many of us let our circumstances and situations dictate how we feel? How often does our inadequacy in one area affect how we view ourselves and what worth we believe we have. We feel ourselves plunging into the depths of failure and defeat. We set expectations for ourselves that no one else has and we try to live up to a standard that we were never designed to keep. Then we punish ourselves because we feel unworthy and ashamed of the mess that we make.

"If I make my bed in the depths, you are there." No matter where we take ourselves and how far we try to push others away there is one that will never be put off when we turn our backs and decide to throw in the towel. Even "in the depths" the Lord is there. Jesus our saviour came *to lift us from the miry clay.* (Psalm 40:2). To remove us from a life of defeat and disappointment and to restore us to wholeness. He came to say you are of immeasurable worth not because of what you do but because of who you are. As a child of God you are significant. And from this place of knowing your value you will find that you are empowered to do significant things for Him.

Let me tell you the end of the Roman story. After re- evaluating her original picture I found my daughter trying desperately to get the creases out of the crumpled page, but to no avail. We chatted and I managed to help her see that if she had done such a good job the first time she was even more than capable of doing an even better job the second time around. With fresh hope in her heart she got started and the final product was brilliant. She got out of the depths and all was right with the world again!

So what are you going to fill your mind with? Don't allow the lies of the enemy to dictate how you see yourself. If you feel yourself going down a spiral of negative thinking that is coming against who God says you are, take the sword of the Spirit, God's word that speaks the truth about what he thinks about you and allow His thoughts to redirect your mind into peace and rest. Wherever you find yourself, you will never be beyond His reach.

13

If I rise on the wings of the dawn

if I settle on the far side of the sea

One of the things I love about the Bible is how beautifully poetic it can be. God's inherent majesty is not only portrayed in the splendour of His creation but also in His ability to inspire creative imagery in His word. The Lord is always wanting to draw us closer, to reveal greater depths of His grandeur. He wants our minds to be on an ever expanding journey as we see each day how awesome He is.

It cannot be revealed in one go because we simply couldn't comprehend it. We will never fully understand or fathom Him fully on this earth but He longs to lead us step by step. He uses every part of our being to try and encapsulate the vastness of His supremacy and power.

"The heavens declare the glory of God;
  the skies proclaim the work of His hands.
  Day after day they pour forth speech;
  night after night they display knowledge.
  There is no speech or language

where their voice is not heard.
Their voice goes out into all the earth,
*their words to the ends of the world."*Psalm(19:1-4)

Everyday the Lord is calling out to every individual who walks this earth to tell them that He is above it all. Every part of creation points to Him. The world that we see is so vast and expansive. The stretches of the African Sahara, the immense landscapes of the Australian outback and the terrific peaks of the Himalayan mountain range are magnificent and yet at the moment we only see in part.

Even the words that are used in the Bible to describe the world are infused with elegance and grace. He is trying to stretch our imaginations, to make us reach further in our thoughts and the mental pictures that we create on the inside. He wants to give us a vision in our inner man which is much bigger than the one we can see with our physical eyes.

Why is it so important that we take time to meditate on everything that the Lord has made? What happens when we don't read about the magnificence of creation and ponder on the brilliance of the Lord? If we do not frame our thinking around the truth we will find that our carnal minds paint a picture of reality that is fed by fear and self -centeredness. Our fleshly thinking can get so small. When our eyes are not looking up and gazing upon the one who is so much bigger than us then we find that our eyes begin to rest on ourselves. We become focused on our issues, our problems, our battles and before we know it situations and circumstances are towering over us. We struggle to know how we will ever be able to find a way out.

Self- occupation will always make our lives small. It limits our ability to see clearly and have a true perspective on a situation. That is why the

Lord gives us these pictures throughout scripture to cause our view to be enlarged and to challenge our glass ceilings.

If I rise on the wings of the dawn, if I settle on the far side of the sea..

The picture created here is that the furthest parts of the earth will not be beyond the reach of our loving Father. No matter how far away we might feel we have drifted, how distracted our thoughts have been and how distant we feel in our hearts, the Lord is with us right now. He has committed Himself to our well-being and He is more than capable of fulfilling His promises towards us. Centre your thoughts on this truth today and allow your mind to be filled with His peace.

14

Even there your hand will guide me

your right hand will hold me fast

The hand is the most frequently used symbol of the body. It is associated with protection, strength, blessing and generosity. We have probably all used the term "to lend a hand" or asked " Can you give me a hand?" We say it when we need help. It's our way of admitting that we can't get by on our own and there are areas of our lives where we need to depend on others. It is a question that will at times require us to humble ourselves and recognise that we need others. We often only ask people who we feel confident will be willing to listen to our request or will be prepared to take action as lending a hand will usually cost something. It will normally require someone to stop what they are focusing on and put their attention on someone else.

There is something personal when someone says they will lend you a hand. They are investing in you, they are engaging with you. The very metaphor itself paints the picture of an intimate connection. Just like when we hold out a hand to help some up or where we reach out a hand to stop someone from falling. A hand signifies friendship, intimacy and trust. Remember what it was like when you were in school and you were asked to hold hands with kids in the line. If you didn't like the person you had been paired with you would be very reluctant to give them your hand. It felt too personal, too close.

The word in Hebrew for hand is yadl. It is associated with not only strength, but with authority and power. It is also significant when the term "right hand" is used. To be at the right side *"is to be identified as being in the special place of honour"* In Jesus' parable of the sheep and the goats, they are separated with the sheep on the right hand of God and the goats on the left hand. We also see how the right hand is used to describe the place of glory and honour in heaven.

After the Lord Jesus had spoken to them, he was taken up into heaven and he sat at the right hand of God. Mark 16:19, and again in Matthew 26: 64 *"But I say to all of you: From now on you will see the Son of Man sitting at the right hand of the Mighty One and coming on the clouds of heaven."*

These verses show us the significance of the right hand. A place where Christ himself sits, the position of highest honour that is above every power and principality. Above all situations and circumstances. Through laying down His life he has now been exalted to that place where He is no longer subject to the forces of this world.

Now this same hand is being extended to each one of us.

Many of us can go through seasons where we can feel like we are drowning. Where we feel like we are in the midst of a raging storm and it seems like we are going to be overwhelmed by the wind and the waves. We are surrounded on every side and we just don't feel like we can keep our heads above water. In these moments we need to hold on to the one who is holding onto us and believe the truth of the word that says " your right hand will hold me fast."

The Lord uses His right hand, that place of greatest strength and highest authority, to reach into your life and take hold of you. His grip does not weaken over time. His hold is not dependent on a strength that can wain. He is the Almighty God. The everlasting one. The Alpha and the Omega. He will be with you to the end. He won't let go of you because His hand has already raised Jesus from the grave and defeated death itself. We are not being held by a tin-pot God. We are in the hands of the greatest super power against which no enemy stands a chance.

The Lord said to my Lord: "Sit at my right hand, until I put your enemies under your feet. Matthew 22:44

Be mindful of this and allow Him to guide you by the hand today.

15

If I say "Surely the darkness will hide me"

and the light become night around me, even the darkness will not be dark to you

A number of years ago we went on holiday to Kerry in the south of Ireland. One of the things that stood out to us the most about the trip was the incredible night sky. With living in the city we are familiar with having lots of lights, so even night time is not particularly dark. We had never experienced a sky absent of all the usual forms of light pollution from houses, cars and street lamps. We mentioned this to people who lived in the area and they told us that where we were staying was on the edge of a "dark sky reserve." This was something that I had never heard of before. It was an area that was totally void of all light pollution. There was no trace of artificial light. The sky was pitch black - except that it wasn't black. The darkness was merely the backdrop for the incredible array of stars that lit up the whole sky every night.

When I was reading this verse I reflected on this. What was called a Dark sky reserve seemed to be a contradiction in terms. When all the artificial light was taken away it was called a dark sky and yet it actually allowed people to see light. The beauty that shone out from the stars was now apparent in a new and exciting way. It was not that the stars suddenly appeared because they had always been there but because of the 'light pollution' from our 21st century lives it was much harder to distinguish them and fully appreciate their majesty and brilliance.

The imagery of darkness and light is used throughout the Bible. When Jesus walked the earth He revealed himself as *the light of the world.* He invited people to follow Him promising that

"Whoever follows me will not walk in darkness, but will have the light of life." John 8:12

When we made that decision to give our lives to the Lord we were changed forever as we read in 1 Peter 2:9 he describes how Jesus called us *"out of darkness into His marvellous light"*. As children of God we will never be overcome by darkness because darkness is a metaphor for death. Jesus went into the tomb, He went to death itself, that place where there is no light hope, or life and he overcame it. We have been lifted out of that place of despair and we are now free to walk as children of light. (Ephesians 5:8)

This doesn't mean that we do not go through times when we feel like we are in a dark place. There can be seasons when we struggle to see things clearly and we don't have a positive picture of the future. We might face real challenges to our health or we might be fighting with worries and anxieties that mean we can't imagine a way forward. In these dark moments we can lose hope on the inside and can convince ourselves that it is better to hide away. We actually want the darkness to surround us and make us invisible. We sometimes even tell ourselves that our lives amount to nothing and that it would be better to withdraw and let ourselves sink back into oblivion.

I love how the Lord brings hope through His word. Look at how he encourages us through these verses: in Psalm 139 *even the darkness will not be dark to you*; No matter what kind of darkness tries to plague your mind, it will never be able to overtake you, because we read in John 1:5 *The light shines in the darkness, and the darkness has not overcome it.* Just like the dark sky reserve actually reveals the light that God has placed in the sky, the dark situations you can at times find yourself in just serve as a backdrop for God to shine the intensity of His love deep into your heart. He can turn the most difficult of experiences into opportunities for you to encounter Him in a new and powerful way. You have a new identity in Him which means you are in this world but no longer of this world. (John 17: 16). Just like a star is positioned above the earth you have been seated with Christ in heavenly places.(Ephesians 2:6)

Meditate on this

For at one time you were darkness, but now you are light in the Lord. 1 Peter 2:9

16

The night will shine like the day for darkness is as light to you

One of my son's greatest strengths and more challenging attributes is the fact that he is incredibly persistent. If he sets his mind on something, you will have a pretty tough job convincing him of another option or that he may not be in possession of all the facts.

One of the things that we look back and laugh at now was when he was doing a topic in maths on conversions. He had been learning about the number of metres in a kilometre. One day we were out where a race was taking place and the people were running 6 miles. We asked the question "I wonder what that distance would be in kilometres?" to which our son answered, "You can't work that out because you can't convert kilometres into miles." We realised that they had not covered this area in school yet and so assured him that he would go on to learn how to convert different ways of measuring as there are about 1.6km in a mile. But he would not accept it. "You're wrong, You've made that up. There is no way of converting kilometres to miles" he said with such confidence.

As a parent you try your best to explain when a child doesn't understand something and you find yourself saying the same information in as many different ways as possible to try and get your message across. But with a person who is very persistent about what they think, and who is convinced they are right, you quickly realise you are wasting your time. He was so determined that it was as if we were trying to convince him white was black. He got really frustrated with us and we just changed the subject and hoped he wasn't going to get an exam question anytime soon askingbabout conversions.

As we grow up in life we learn that there are things that are fluid, those things that can adapt and change, and there are things that are concrete. There are hard facts and there are opinions. The incredible truth about our journey with the Lord is that what we can often view as hard facts can actually be subject to change in the spirit realm. What do I mean by this? When we look at the Bible we find time and time again stories that defy the notion of what possible.

In the Old Testament we see how Moses reaches out His staff and the waters of the Red sea are pushed back and the children of Israel find a way through. Next these same people find themselves in the desert with no water but Moses strikes a rock and water runs from it. Then the people are afraid they will starve as there is no food, but when Moses seeks God He rains down food from heaven.

On each of these occasions they are faced with an impossible situation. Each time they believe they have come to the end of the road. When they find themselves in a dark place the Lord's love shines in and brings an answer.

That is what the Lord does for us. He steps into our world when there is confusion and we can only see it one way. Where the world says there is no other option He says "I see it differently. You are only seeing in part. Your picture is incomplete." The Lord comes to challenge our thinking and to get us to take the limits off what we believe He can do. He is above every situation and everything is subject to Him. *"the night will shine like the day for darkness is as light to you."* What we see as certain and unchanging He can turn around in an instant. What we see as rigid and something we have to learn to live with, He sees as an opportunity to show you His glory and power.

I realise that we actually need to be a bit more like our son. To have that same tenacity. To look at things and no matter how many people are telling you it can only go one way, to actually be so convinced of the goodness of God that you back what He says. To get to that place fill your mind with His truth and stand on His promises. That is the only way the impossible becomes possible.

17

For you created my inmost being

you knit me together in my mother's womb

A young couple in our church have recently had their first child. They have impressively made it out to church with their newborn on a number of occasions which any parent will know deserves a medal! One thing I have noticed when they arrive is that everyone is drawn to them. Their beautiful wee son is like a magnet. He literally attracts people from all over the room. Everyone is fascinated by his tiny hands, his wrinkled forehead and delicate smile. He is just a wonder.

I realise that we can often get caught up in life and miss out on the awe of who we are and the miracle of life itself. I read this quote by the theologian Augustine who lived in the 4th century.

"Men go abroad to wonder at the heights of mountains, at the huge waves of the sea, at the long courses of the rivers, at the vast compass of the ocean, at the circular motions of the stars; and they pass by themselves without wondering."

It takes the presence of a baby to remind us again of the mystery of it all. How as human beings we can produce something so perfect, so intricate and so incredible. I remember back to the days when my kids were first born and how we just used to sit and stare at them and marvel at God's goodness in our lives.

I love the words that are used in this verse: *you knit me together in my mother's womb.* This gives us the picture of how we are so carefully crafted. Knitting speaks of a tender art form, made by hand. Stitch by stitch. Have you ever wondered why God did it this way? Why did he take His time?

In my opinion, there are a number of reasons why the Lord chose for mother and baby to go through the 9 month journey. Firstly, the Lord wants us to recognise that there is no part of us that he rushed over. Everything is purposefully created with His unique design. We have been well thought out. We are not an accident or insignificant. Every part of who we are has been conceived by God.

Secondly, we were made in secret. A time so precious that not even our earthly mothers could see it. They had to trust in faith that the work was being done. They had signs of growth but they couldn't see with their eyes. They could only imagine and paint a picture of what the future could look like. During the waiting time the parents dream and hope, using their imagination to envisage a new life. This is a God given ability and during this time God is stirring in every heart a new excitement and expectation for life.

Thirdly, I believe it is an opportunity for God to reveal His glory. For all parents, no matter how smart we are, or how much we believe we have things together, we can never explain away the magnificence of new life.

It is beyond words. It makes us dumbstuck and it humbles us. I believe every parent must at some point ask themselves "How is this possible?"

What is also interesting about these verses in Psalm 139, is that before the Lord even talks about how we are knitted together, which most of us would associate with the growth and development of our physical bodies, the psalmists begin by saying " *You created my inmost being.*" This shows us that God made you who you are. You have been given a unique personality, gifting and potential. That inner part of us that no one else can ever truly know and see is what God designed and brought into being. At that embryonic stage he was fashioning into being the very essence of what makes you your unique self. He thought about every piece of you. He dreamt about you and then gave those thoughts substance and life. He spoke possibility over you. He spoke promise over you gave you the inherent capacity to be a channel of His blessing and life.

I believe this was such an invaluable time for the Lord to enjoy creating us and calling forth all that he saw us to be. We have been formed by the hands of God. He breathes His life into us. He is working with us, shaping us with His hands into vessels that will bring Him glory. The world may not see you as you truly are but God sees you as the final product! Allow your mind to be expanded by this truth today.

18

I praise you because I am fearfully and wonderfully made

your works are wonderful, I know that full well.

Have you ever thought about how often you praise God and thank Him for your life and for everything that makes you your unique self? So much of our culture is based on self improvement. We are always encouraged to think about how we can become better versions of ourselves. I am not against people developing themselves or thinking about how they can grow. What I am beginning to realise though is that, in order to grow, it is important we know where we are starting from.

Too many of us are starting from a place of low self-worth. In our attempts to grow we have placed too great an emphasis on what we can't do and have become overly fixated on our weaknesses. Whether it is to do with how we look, how smart we are, how well we cope with social situations or how good we are at stewarding our finances, we tend to magnify the gaps and pass over the areas where we feel more confident.

When this occurs we are left with this nagging sense that we are never quite good enough. We will never really meet the mark. We see some improvements but it always feels like we have a long way to go. I don't believe this is the way the Lord designed it to be. He wants us to grow, but not because we are not yet good enough. He wants us to be on this journey of grace upon grace where we walk into greater levels of authority and influence. He wants our eyes are opened to the potential He has put on the inside of us and the opportunities that He wants us to take hold of and embrace.

This should not be an uphill struggle where we try in our own efforts to be something while underneath we fear we will never have what it takes. We need to recognise where we are starting from. We are already the full package. We can give thanks and celebrate right now who we are because the Father, through Jesus, has already perfected us.

We are "fearfully and wonderfully made" The word *wonderfully* comes from the Hebrew Palah and it means *"to be distinct, marked out, to be separated or to be distinguished."* This is why we praise Him. We have already been set apart for His purposes. He has a divine assignment for which he has equipped us and given us everything we need. The word tells us

For if, by the trespass of the one man, death reigned through that one man, how much more will those who receive God's abundant provision of grace and of the gift of righteousness reign in life through the one man, Jesus Christ. Romans 5:17

Many of our attempts to better ourselves are driven by a need to be significant. We have been created with an inert desire for purpose and destiny. We want to make our lives count. However we are not supposed to carry the weight of this. When we trust Him and allow His spirit to lead us and His word to be magnified in our lives we will start to unlock the potential he has placed within us.

We don't have to try and get noticed. We don't need to shout the loudest or be the smartest or look the best. The Lord has set us apart. We will stand out for Him and reveal His glory because that is what we have been created to do. It's part of the calling on our lives. Simply by communing with the Lord and resting in His love we will find that we will radiate His life to those around us.

So where should our focus be? Where can we direct our thoughts? The Lord has already made us significant. Now we just need to align our hearts to this truth and declare it over our lives.

19

My frame was not hidden from you

*when I was made in the secret place, when I was
woven together in the depths of the earth.*

We are blessed with 3 amazing kids and we are so thankful for them (nearly all of the time!!). They add so much colour and fun to our lives and keep us on our toes. Our journey to having a family however was not as straightforward as we would have hoped. There was a time when we wondered if we would ever have children. There were periods of waiting both before our first son was born, and then again between our son and first daughter. This means that there is a 6 year gap between our first two kids.

My son, over the years, has repeatedly told me "This wasn't a good idea Mum. What were you thinking?!" Everytime his younger sisters annoyed him or interrupted his plans because it was nap time or they needed to go to bed early he would become extremely frustrated with our lack of forethought. Why couldn't he have siblings closer to his age? Why did he end up with two younger sisters?

The truth is we don't have all the answers. All I knew through that period of our lives was that God is good and there was no good thing that he would withhold from us. So we kept praying and believing that he would give us the desires of our heart for a family. Whenever I became pregnant I remember how we tried to imagine what they would be like. Who would they look like? Who would they take after? Would they be outgoing like their Dad? Would they be sensitive like their Mum? Would they be bossy? (I'm not saying who that would be like!) During that time we couldn't see with our eyes. We had to trust and believe that God was creating this most incredible gift for us.

When our kids are young many of us make plans for them and think about what we want to see in their future. We might make it our aim to ensure they have the opportunities we never had, or we might think about all that our parents did for us and aspire to do the same. We perhaps believe that it's a good education, a strong friendship group or plenty of outside interests that will be the secret to their success and happiness in life.

What I understand more and more as I watch my kids grow up is that my hopes and dreams for them can at times limit their potential. My thoughts, although coming from a desire to bless and prosper them, will not necessarily be what will release them into the abundant life that God has for them. As I meditate on psalm 139 I realise that everything about them has been uniquely designed by the Lord to equip them to fulfil His mission for them on this earth. There is no part of their makeup that was ill thought out or done by chance. Even the very hour they entered the world was known by the Lord. The place where they are born was specially chosen.

When the Lord was creating each one of us He did it with such care and love. Everyone of us was significant to the Lord before anyone even knew of our existence. Have you ever taken a moment to stop and think about this? You were in God's mind way before you were even conceived. If you struggle to believe this, read it for yourself.

"Before I formed you in the womb I knew you, before you were born I set you apart; I appointed you as a prophet to the nations." Jeremiah 1:5

Before we became a physical being we had been conceived in the heart of our heavenly Father. Everything that is experienced in the natural world comes first from the spiritual realm. There was a time when who we were was hidden, not known by man, but we were cherished and loved by the Lord. In that secret place of intimacy He formed us and made awesome plans for our lives. He appointed us and our children for this time and place in history. Whenever we are plagued with thoughts that we don't matter, that we are insignificant, that our kids won't make it or that they don't have what they need to succeed in life, come back to these verses.

The Lord has poured out who He is into each one of us. He has fashioned us and shaped us *for such a time as this.*

20

Your eyes saw my unformed body

Are there times when you feel unnoticed? Are there moments when you are wondering if anyone is actually listening to what you have to say? Many of us can go through periods of struggling with thoughts of inadequacy or we question whether our contribution is valued or taken seriously by others.

If you feel like you are having to try and get someone's attention just stop right now and rest in the fact that you already have the attention of the most important person you will ever meet. The Lord has had His eyes on you for a very long time. You have been under His watchful gaze from before time began. His eyes saw you before you were even conceived.

This may feel too difficult to comprehend so in order for it to make sense to us we need to go back to the beginning and read about how God operates.

One of the incredible things about creation is the fact that it was spoken into being. We see from the very first verses in the Bible how God took the darkness and void and when He spoke light came forth. God shows us this pattern of how he operates to help us walk by faith and not by sight. God has the power to fashion and design and then bring His creations into existence through the power of His words. In His mind's eye He imagined what His world would look like, what it would be made up of, how it would look and then He declared that it would be so.

We read on in Genesis that when we were created we were made in the image of God. We reflect His glory. Everything about our bodies shows the fingerprints of a master creator. There are times I like to do a bit of research just to remind myself about the awesome capacity I have been given as a human being. Let me share just the tip of the ice-berg with you to start to expand your thinking.

Your brain's storage capacity is considered virtually unlimited. Research suggests the human brain consists of about 86 billion neurons. Each neuron forms connections to other neurons, which could add up to 1 quadrillion (1,000 trillion) connections.* Over time, these neurons can combine, increasing storage. We are constantly having to update computers and systems because we run out of storage and yet we have this unlimited capacity within our own bodies!

Want another amazing fact? The human brain can generate about 23 watts of power (enough to power a lightbulb!). I don't know about you but we seem to spend our lives constantly searching the house for chargers to keep the many electronic devices that we have in a usable state. They are supposed to make our lives easier and yet we are sitting with such huge latent potential in our minds.

What I find even more exciting is the fact that the Bible tells us in 1 Corinthians 2:16 that we have the mind of Christ. What an amazing statement! We have access to ways of thinking that are beyond intellect and natural human intelligence. We have wisdom and insight that is supernatural. We can tap into the resources of heaven and believe for thinking that will cure diseases, push to new levels in technologies and inventions and will demonstrate creativity in music and the arts that leaves people standing in awe.

The devil might try to persuade you that you are not important and that you don't have much to offer. But come against his lies with the truth. Before you became "real" in the world's eyes the Lord had already destined you for purpose and significance. He saw you, He dreamt about you and He spoke your life into existence. Now embrace who He says you are and discover all that He has for you!

References: Stunning details of the brain. https://www.sciencedaily.com/

21

All the days ordained for me

were written in your book before one of them came to be

Would you describe yourself as a planner or would you be more of a spontaneous type of person? I am definitely on the planner side of the fence, which has its advantages and its drawbacks. The advantages are you will never find yourself on a trip or day out with me and go hungry. I am renowned for making sure there are plenty of supplies to see us through. In fact my kids were so conditioned to there always being plenty of snacks that I couldn't even take them to the park for an hour without them expecting a whole packed lunch.

That's the positive side of planning. The negative side would be felt by all those who have to live with me. My husband would have more of a laissez-faire approach to life. He hates to be too hemmed in with details, arrangements and deadlines. It got to the stage where he would dread opening His eyes on a saturday morning for fear of all the things I had organised in my head for the day to come. Needless to say after 25 years of marriage I have learned to tone it down and he has learned to be a bit more proactive. I now find him writing lists and sending himself reminders while I can leave the house without a care in the world, or bag of snacks – much to my kids dismay!

Having a plan for our lives is an issue that we all grapple with. There are times when we wonder what the big plan is. We can go through seasons where we are focused on goals and motivated about achieving them. Then there are other periods of our lives where we feel like we are drifting or we don't feel like we are moving at all. It can seem like we are simply going through the motions, replaying the same scenes everyday and not having a sense that anything is changing or ever will.

I have had moments when I have cried out to the Lord and asked "What is this all about?" "What happened to all the dreams that you put in my heart?" Somehow where I expected to be at this stage in my life is not lining up to where I find myself. My plan looked different. In my eyes I was maybe more successful or more "together" – whatever that means. I realise when I look at myself through the lens of the world and through its estimation of what achievement looks like, I can quickly feel like I'm falling short.

This is why it is so important that we uncover the truth of who we are and fill our minds with the thoughts that the Lord feels has about us.

Jesus revealed himself to the disciples in the book of John as the good shepherd. One of the main roles of the shepherd is to guide and protect the sheep. He goes before them leading the way. He takes them to places where they can feed and rest. He reaches out and helps them when they are in danger.

We might wonder where we are going in life but we need to understand that if we are staying close to the shepherd he will ensure that we get to where we need to go. We may feel like we are straying off but we are never out of His watchful eye. He is always coming alongside us to tenderly nudge us in the right direction. We might not always see the big picture but the Lord sees the beginning and the end. We may go through a season where we fail to understand why we are taking a certain route, but we will one day look back and know how the Lord proved His faithfulness and love. Other times He will teach us about the potential that he has put on the inside of us that we just couldn't see if we hadn't walked through that challenge or overcome that obstacle.

Your life might not follow your plan but be sure of this promise everyday.

He will feed His flock like a shepherd. He will carry the lambs in His arms, holding them close to His heart. Isaiah 40:11

22

How precious to me are your thoughts, God

How vast is the sum of them!

D o you ever have moments when someone asks you what you are thinking and you reply "Nothing"? Often it is not that our heads are empty but instead our minds have lots of thoughts and ideas whirling around. We may find ourselves day dreaming and jumping from one thought to another. We consider options, imagine possibilities and wrestle with doubts.

Science tells us we can have up to 60,000 thoughts a day and yet there are many times when we can struggle to clearly articulate even one of them. We are constantly being stimulated by sights and sounds which open up new paths to us. Situations trigger memories that make us remember people and places in the past. Our inner world is a hive of activity where we relive experiences, imagine future opportunities or think about how to respond to what is right in front of us.

We have been created with an incredible capacity to think and our thought life is extremely active. Many people struggle to control their thoughts finding themselves thinking about things that cause them to feel anxious or stressed. Most psychologists will highlight the links between our thought lives and our emotions. When we think on particular things it will influence how we feel, and then that can play out in our behaviours. When our minds are dominated by negative thoughts we end up feeling that we are being held captive by recurring thinking patterns that limit our success.

Our capacity to think is a God given gift. He gave us this ability because we have been made in His image. He is the creator of all original thought and He has a lot to say about what we think on because He knows how powerful it is.

Finally, brothers and sisters, whatever is true, whatever is noble, whatever is right, whatever is pure, whatever is lovely, whatever is admirable—if anything is excellent or praiseworthy—think about such things. Philippians 4:8

God only wants our minds to be fixed on good things because he knows that when we dwell on this we will see it play out in our lives.

"For as he thinks in His heart, so is he." Proverbs 23:7

When we think on what is good and we consider it, ponder it and imagine it, we will begin to see this as our reality. Why is this? We are coming into agreement with the way of the Kingdom. We are inviting the domain of heaven to be part of the reality that we see on the earth.

One of the things I love about psalm 139 is the fact that we learn about the vast sum of thought that the Lord has concerning us. Often when someone tells us they were thinking about us we ask ourselves

2 questions. Are they happy with us or have I done something wrong? We either feel touched to know that someone cares or we feel under the spotlight.

When it comes to God's thoughts about us I think for the most part we can often find ourselves leaning towards the second option. If we have had negative experiences of authority figures in our lives we can then relate to the Lord in this way. We feel like when He looks at us he focuses on our lack and the areas where we fail to measure up. We imagine God as being disapproving or disappointed. This is where we need to remind ourselves that God is love. It is not that He has to choose to be loving, He is love itself and He cannot operate outside of His nature. When he says " Whatever is lovely, *whatever is admirable—if anything is excellent or praiseworthy —think about such things.*" This is how He sees you. He sees you as perfect and righteous because Jesus has paid the price for all your sin and failure. You are a new creation and God is pleased with the work of His hands. His thoughts about you are only good. Take some time and make sure this truth is filling your mind today!

23

Were I to count them

they would outnumber the grains of sand

I t seems to me there are two types of people in life. Those who love the beach and those who hate it. For some people lying in the sun, hearing the sound of the waves gently lapping on the shore feels like heaven, whereas others dread the thought of having to set foot on it. I would be someone who enjoys a day by the sea and having a picnic but I have to admit you find yourself in a constant battle with a certain substance that appears to get everywhere. Sand! It gets in your hair. It gets stuck between your toes and despite your best efforts to keep your hands clean you somehow find yourself eating crunchy sandwiches. I think the worst thing was when my kids were young and having to try and rub sun cream on them before they managed to get caked in sand. Or to stop them from rolling in it just after you had plastered them from head to toe with factor 50.

Then there's leaving the beach and trying your best not to take it home with you in the car. No matter how many times you bang or brush your shoes and how many ways you shake your towel you can guarantee that when you get home your car is covered with tiny little particles which you still haven't managed to get rid of by the next summer.

The incredible thing is that no matter how much sand we appear to have taken with us, or how many impressive monuments we have built with 100's of buckets full of the stuff, when we look back at the beach it never appears to be any different. There is still an abundance of yellow as far as the eye can see.

I remember when my kids were younger they would set themselves the challenge of digging the biggest hole on the beach. They would join forces to take on the sand and see if they could get to the bottom where the sand ran out. Obviously as parents you love it when your kids occupy themselves for hours on end allowing you to enjoy some peace in the sun.

Whether kids or adults we all see that there is what appears to be a limitless amount of sand on the earth. It would never cross our minds that we would turn up to find an empty beach. Can you imagine your kids throwing their buckets down and saying there's no sand. It's all gone!

That is what makes it so powerful when the Lord uses this picture of the sand to communicate His heart towards us. None of us would ever dream of trying to count grains of sand. Even times when I could trick my kids into doing silly time wasting games I was never able to get them to participate in this one. "Off you go and count the grains of sand out there." They would just look at you as if you were crazy. Even saying go and fill your little bucket with sand and start with that wouldn't have made it anymore plausible. We know it's impossible. We can't begin to be able to quantify something which is so vast and beyond our ability to measure.

And yet the Lord wants us to use our imaginations to try and begin to understand the depth of His love and care towards us. Even though it is something so unfathomable, so incomprehensible he wants us to have a go and stretch our hearts and minds a little so that we can expand our capacity to receive from Him.

You see when you are on the beach the one thing I learnt quickly is that if you want to build a big castle, you will need the biggest bucket and spade. Our kids always seemed to end up fighting over this. The bigger the bucket, the bigger the tower. Thinking on this has made me realise that the Lord wants us to come to Him daily with a big bucket. The largest one we can find because when we do He will fill it. His love and devotion towards us is beyond our imagination but if we keep receiving from Him we are able to slowly build a picture of what this is like.

24

When I awake, I am still with you

When we had our first baby I remember sitting next to the Moses basket watching him as he slept. He looked so peaceful and content. Just being able to sit beside him and see him gently breathing felt relaxing. For the first few months he slept in the same room as us at night but I remember the big transition when we moved him into his own room. This seemed like such a big deal. You almost felt like you were abandoning him. Leaving such a little, helpless soul to make it through the night on their own.

At that time we had a baby monitor that we could set up in His room. I can still hear my parents and in-laws saying "there was nothing like that in our day." In their heads this was all a bit over the top. "If they need something they will let you know." was their attitude. They couldn't understand why we would jump up each time we heard a little sniffle. In fairness you realise that God knew what he was doing when he created a baby. They may be small but they can certainly make a loud noise and let you know if they're not happy!

Now my kids are older and when they go to bed each night we don't even think about it. We don't run if we hear them sneeze or cough. We know they can come and find us if they need anything. However there was a night recently when our youngest daughter awoke feeling very unwell. She was burning hot and when we checked her temperature it was 40.2 degrees. We called the doctor and they told us to use some well know paediatric medicine. My husband and I were both alarmed and when we went to see if we had any medicine to bring her temperature down we found we had run out. We were then searching for a 24 hour pharmacy. When we finally got the medicine and Sophie settled down she fell asleep next to me and I lay beside her to make sure she was ok.

I was suddenly taken back to those days of listening to the monitor. As she lay beside me I could hear her taking each breath. Something that I just took for granted any other time was now on my mind. Is she ok? Is she breathing steadily? What was her body fighting? I was mindful of her every move and was concerned when she was restless or unsettled. In the morning when she woke up I was already awake watching her.

Suddenly I was hit by the incredible revelation that what I had just done was what the Lord did for me and my whole family every night. He tells us in Psalm 139 that he is always with us, that He is ever present. We go about our days, we think about Him and let's be honest at times our minds are elsewhere, but He is constant in His commitment to us. Our relationship with Him is two way, but whereas we fail to be consistent in our contact and connection, He is always keeping up His end of the bargain.

I often find myself falling into bed after a busy day. There are times I am mindful of the Lord and how he has sustained me, blessed me and brought me through. There are other times I have allowed myself to run on empty and I have crawled into bed, hoping that a good night's sleep will get me recharged so that I can face the next day. What I frequently fail to remember is that even during those hours of stillness, where I have checked out and switched off, the Lord has never taken His eyes off me. Every breath, every stirring, not just in my physical body but in my mind and my heart, the Lord is has watched over.

Watching Sophie as she rested brought this to life for me in technicolour. When she opened her eyes to face a new day I was there to see how she was. I was on hand to get her anything she needed and to encourage her that I was taking care of her. How many of us need to adjust our thinking to line up with how the Lord feels about us at the beginning of each day. Too often when we open our eyes we are reminded of demands, or the areas we are lacking in. Our heads can be filled with everything that we think we need to do and thoughts that somehow we will not be enough. The problem is we are looking to ourselves rather than looking to the one who has been watching over us and giving us our every breath.

Turn your thinking today towards the Lord and allow His tender mercy to flood your day with hope and peace. He is your very present help from the moment you open your eyes to the moment you lay down your head and all the moments in between.

25

If only you, God, would slay the wicked

Away from me, you who are bloodthirsty!
They speak of you with evil intent, your adversaries misuse your name.

I f only. They are two interesting words. These six little letters could appear so small that you hardly need to take any notice of them and yet they are so powerful.

How many of us have found ourselves paralysed in life because we have got stuck going around the same mountain of "If only..". We have churned over the endless opportunities that could have arisen *if only* we had, or hadn't chosen a particular path. We end up torturing ourselves as we imagine all the scenarios that could have been but weren't.

If only I had stayed at home. *If only* I had spoken up. *If only* I had taken the job. *If only* I had asked for help. We can get ourselves so stuck in the past and what might have been that we can't seem to see a new way forward.

We not only get frustrated with ourselves but we often get frustrated with others. *If only they*.... How often do we fall into the trap of believing that our destiny is determined by others? How often have we given control of our lives to other people? *If only they* had asked me how I was doing. *If only they* had thought about what I needed. *If only they*...Again we can think of 100's of ways others could have stepped up and stepped into our worlds to help us when we needed it. Life could have been so different.

Then there's the *if only you*. The one that is directed to God himself.

If only you. Many times when we go through challenges and trials we begin to question where God is. We start to ask ourselves why would a good God allow me to go through this. Why would He allow people to treat me in this way? Why would I be afflicted by this sickness? Why would I suffer with my finances when I have been so faithful in giving? Why would I experience rejection when I have only tried to love others? We can allow lies to come in about God's character. Does He not care? Does He not want to help me?

In today's verse we see how David calls out to the Lord. He is not doubting the Lord's love towards him, but he is confused as to why the Lord will not deal with the wickedness he sees around him. David knows that the Lord can see those who are doing evil. Why then does He not "slay the wicked?"

The answer lies in all the verses of the Psalm that we have read so far. He made us and He knows us. Each and everyone of us. Whether we acknowledge Him or not we are His precious creation and His heart longs for us to choose to give our lives to Him. So whereas we like to jump in and deal with whatever it is that we don't like, the Lord is endlessly patient. He is in it for the long haul. He will walk the journey with His people throughout their lives.

That is why He sent Jesus. The saviour of the world. he did this to show a world that had turned upon itself that it will never be free until it surrenders and asks for help. Some people will accept the invitation. Some will continue to walk in darkness. Through David's line would come the son of God. The Messiah would finally set the people free and to bring them into the light.

When you are tempted to give up on some of those around you, pause for a second and remember the grace that has been poured out into your own life. You did nothing to deserve it. It was freely given as a gift. Now find someone who you can share that gift with and call them up to discover their true identity as a child of God.

26

Do I not hate those who hate you, Lord

and abhor those who are in rebellion against you?
I have nothing but hatred for them; I count them my enemies.

W hen David walked the earth he had to stand up against the physical enemies of God. He was the young man that dared to come face to face with the giant Goliath who had paralysed the entire nation of Israel in fear. David stood in the face of danger and defied the taunts from Goliath. He rose up with righteous indignation because he saw that this was not simply a mere man that Goliath was challenging, but it was the name and honour of His God and Lord. He was prepared to put His life on the line in order to face down the evil threats of a people that stood in rebellion against His God.

It was not that David believed he was strong. David had learned that His God was stronger than any enemy he would have to face. He had seen God's faithfulness many times out in the fields where he had fought the lion and the bear during his time as a shepherd watching his fathers sheep. These lessons had shown him that he could depend on the Lord to save and deliver him when there was danger ahead. He had grown in courage and boldness so that when he was faced with a bigger challenge he remembered past victories. From those he summoned up new confidence and was propelled forward to action. David committed His life to confronting those things that came against him in opposition to God.

When Jesus came to walk the earth He brought a new message. He showed mankind that we no longer fight a physical battle where we come against people. the nature of the battle changed. It is now a spiritual one. The better news is that when Jesus came to the earth He came to fight this spiritual battle on our behalf. He came to defeat the works of the enemy. The devil's greatest plan to destroy mankind was foiled at the cross where Jesus

"Having disarmed principalities and powers, .. made a public spectacle of them, triumphing over them..." Col 2:15

Jesus took every charge that the enemy could hold against us and He paid the price for us. He brought us out of captivity and into freedom. He made a way for us to live a victorious life in which we can enjoy His presence and His peace. The one thing we need to be mindful of is the fact that we are still living in a fallen world. We are not called to fight people, we are called to stand against the powers and principalities that seek to wreak havoc on the earth. They will do everything they can to challenge our belief in the Father's love. They will seek to put doubts in our minds about the goodness of God and will put obstacles in our path that will attempt to hinder us from receiving all that God has promised us.

The great news is that God's word tells us we are more than conquerors. I have quoted that verse many times when I have encountered trials and tribulations but, I have only recently received revelation about how powerful it is. We think of a conqueror as being at the highest place of strength. The person who has taken on their enemy and who has come out victorious. So what could be better than this? Why does the Lord say that we are *more than conquerors*? What position is He talking about that is even higher than the person who has won the battle?

To understand what the Lord is talking about we need to turn to the book of Ephesians . In chapter 2 v 6 we read

'*For he raised us from the dead along with Christ and* **seated us** *with Him in the heavenly realms because we are united with Christ Jesus."*

The greatest place of triumph is not battling and overcoming the enemy but resting and trusting that the enemy has already been defeated. This is the position the Lord now wants us to adopt in life. The only fight we have to face is the fight of faith. It is the internal battle in our minds to bring every thought captive to the obedience of Christ in order to allow the reality of heaven to become real in our lives.

What I am beginning to understand is when the enemy comes against me, it is not that I need to respond in fear and begin to panic about what he could steal from me. It is actually just a sign that the devil is already responding in fear as he sees the anointing and potential that the Lord has placed on my life. His attempts to bring me down should actually propel me higher into the destiny that the Lord has ordained for me.

27

Search me, God, and know my heart

D o you ever have times when someone asks you if you're doing okay and you say yes when everything inside is saying no? Or are there moments when you don't really know how you are doing? You may feel a little unsettled but you don't really know why. Our emotions can change many times throughout the day or we can experience prolonged seasons of struggling to keep our heads up and maintain a sense of hope about the future.

One of the difficulties we face is that it takes time to really figure out what is going on in our internal worlds. For us to truly understand ourselves or for other people to get to the bottom of what is bothering us will not be achieved in a casual five minute exchange. We need to pause. We need to reflect. We need space to think. We need to stop and capture those thoughts that are whirling around in our heads. Sometimes they are very obvious because no matter what we do we can't seem to be able to drown them out. We wake up in the middle of the night thinking about them. Other times they are more subtle. They whisper into our minds, like a little splinter that we know is on our finger but we just can't seem to get it out. There's a dull pain but when pressure is put on it we are more aware that it's still there.

These are the reasons we say we are "fine." It's not that we are lying, it's just we don't really know what else to say. We know something is bothering us but we're not really sure what and more importantly if we did know we wouldn't necessarily know how to fix it.

You can have hope today because God is not in a rush when it comes to your well being. He has all the time it will take to help you find the healing that you need for the hurt and disappointment from your past. He values you enough to engage with you everyday and remind you of your incredible worth. You do not need to worry about the Lord searching your heart. He does not judge you on anything other than the work of grace. Many things go through our hearts yet not one of them changes His love for us. When He examines you He declares you pure and acceptable. There is nothing that can ever change that.

We can be impatient with ourselves and often we get impatient with others. There have been many people who have lost patience with me as well. You can have confidence today because the Lord never gets impatient with us. He takes the time that we need to walk the journey. When we read His Word it's like taking a spiritual bath. The things that are making us feel unclean are washed away and we are reminded of the fact that God has made us brand new. Many times we are carrying weights and burdens in our hearts that we are not even aware of. We believe we have upset people, disappointed people or we can even think that God is angry with us. We have a nagging sense of somehow just not quite being good enough and then we allow this lens to shape all the interactions that we have with others.

The Lord is attentive towards us. He searches us not because He wants to find fault with us. He does not search us to show us our lack and where we are going wrong. He searches us because He wants to free our hearts from hurt and pain and restore us to a place where we know that we are loved and accepted.

28

Test me and know my anxious thoughts

God has created us for openness and transparency. He wants us to be able to come to Him and feel that we can share everything that is going on in our lives. The things that we are doing, the way that we are feeling and the thoughts that we are having. The Lord desires for us to be real because He created us for intimacy with Him. Each one of us has that deep longing in our hearts to be true and authentic. To be known and accepted for who we are. Jesus told us He is the truth and we are made in His image. We are hardwired to live lives that are based on being our true selves.

Unfortunately though we mix up how we feel and think about ourselves as sometimes being the truth of who we are. We may feel like we are a loser or a failure. We may feel like we have messed up and made bad choices. We may think we are incapable of change. This may feel very real to us. These thoughts might dominate our minds but we need to remind ourselves that thoughts are not facts. Even when they are strong and feel almost impossible to shake, that does not make them true.

When we came to Christ we were born again, or some translations say we are born from above. This means that God no longer sees us with all our failings and weaknesses; He sees us as a brand new person because His Spirit has come to transform us. Our journey now is to understand who we have become and to live from this new identity.

This is why it is so important that we can be real with the Lord. He doesn't want us to pretend we are feeling worthy and loved if we are feeling unworthy and unlovable. He wants us to come to Him and be honest about our struggles with believing in our new identity. He wants us to learn new things about ourselves by showing us what we now look like as children of God.

He isn't trying to test us to catch us out but at times He will allow us to walk through trying situations in order to reveal to us the places in our thinking where we are holding on to a lie. It might be that you are promoted to work with a new team but although you are happy to accept the challenge everyday you are being plagued by the same nagging thought that somehow they all think you are not quite good enough. It feels like your mind just keeps playing the same phrase that *one day you will be found out. You're not as smart as they think you are.*

Before the promotion you felt confident about your abilities but now that you have stepped out and stepped up into something new you feel shaken. Who you believed yourself to be is suddenly being rocked. This is where the Lord wants to pinpoint the anxious thoughts going off in your head that are now affecting your heart. He wants you to take note of this and bring it to Him. Then you can recognise that it is a lie because it doesn't line up with what the Lord says about you. Once you capture that thought you can reject it and replace it with the truth of His word.

You can do all things through Christ who strengthens you. This is the truth about your ability as a child of the King. You have the resources of heaven at your disposal and the mind of Christ to give you the wisdom and insight you will need. God calls us to walk with Him and learn from Him. He tells us that His yoke is easy and His burden is light. This means that He will only lead us into those positions for which he has equipped us. We won't be overwhelmed and though we have challenges we won't fail. We can trust Him for everything that we need.

The Lord wants you to surrender all your anxious thoughts to Him. You were never designed to have thoughts of inadequacy swirling around in your mind. Instead the Lord wants to expand your mind to the incredible potential and gifting that He has placed on the inside of you and for you to have confidence in how He will use you for His glory.

Whenever you begin to feel your mind straying away from the truth and being bombarded by negative thoughts, confront them with the truth of who the Lord says you are and what He believes about you.

29

See if there is any offensive way in me

A re there times when you know you need to have an honest conversation with someone but you keep putting it off because you are afraid of the consequences? Many of us struggle to be up front and would prefer to live with our frustrations rather than talk it out. Have you ever stopped to wonder why this is? For most of us we are concerned that our relationships won't be strong enough. We believe that if we are truthful we could cause offence to the other person and our friendship might be permanently damaged.

I think what I am realising as I get older is that I feel more comfortable with the people who are upfront with me. I prefer to know what they are really thinking. If they don't give it to me straight I can usually sense that they are not happy and then I begin to speculate about what I have done. That often leads me into a much worse place mentally as I try to figure out how I might have hurt them and what I did or didn't say.

The fact is we all have blind spots. No matter how much we might try to live a life of love towards others, we are imperfect people and we will doubtlessly mess up many times in our relationships. We will naturally see things a certain way. We are influenced by our upbringing, education, culture and experiences. All these things are good and they have help shape who we have become. However they also create a bias in certain areas. We will have filters on the way that we see things and they will at times help us and other times be a hinderance.

I have found over the last number of years I have become much more self-aware. I am learning to reflect more and try not to react so quickly to situations. I am a work in progress. Often when I think I am moving forward I can be confronted with an issue that I thought no longer bothered me and I find myself getting riled and upset.

When David asks the Lord to see if there is any offensive way in him I believe it was because he had tasted how good it was to draw close to God and he didn't want anything to hinder that intimate connection he enjoyed. In the Old testament before Jesus' work on the cross, the people knew that their disobedience had an impact on their standing with the Lord. They couldn't confidently expect to receive from the Lord when they sinned.

Doesn't this make us thankful for everything that Jesus has done for us! What I love the most about my journey with the Lord is that I have come to learn about His patience and His constant care for my well being and development as His child. There is nothing that prevents us from receiving God's fullest expression of love and forgiveness. All our offensive behaviour was dealt with by Jesus at the cross. There is no anger of frustration on His part when I trip up or slip back into old ways. He is not disappointed or irritated. The longing in His heart is simply that I will walk further into the freedom He bought for me.

Interestingly it's not our actions that are our greatest barrier to living a

God empowered life. It's our thoughts and beliefs about who we are and what we can receive as God's child. This is why I still pray David's prayer. In the same way as I want to know if I am inadvertently annoying those around me and causing hurt or pain, I also want the Lord to highlight to me where I might be harbouring bitterness, or jealousy, pride or anger. I would rather have these issues brought into the light and have the lies exposed that are keeping me stuck in cycles of defeat. I understand that having these offensive ways brought out into the open will not mean that the Lord will suddenly love or accept me more. Jesus has already accepted me before I even knew that I was in need of help. But I know when the light comes in the darkness has to flee.

Recently my daughter and I were weeding in the garden. I turned to see that she had cleared a whole patch much quicker than me. I wondered why she was so quick and then I realised that she was just pulling out the leaves. She wanted to get the job done quickly. I was in it for the long haul. I was going for the roots because experience has shown me I will be out here again in another few weeks if I don't invest the time now.

You can have great confidence today that the Lord is 100% invested in you. Your future is more important to Him than you could ever imagine. We might feel frustrated at times when we think we are making very slow progress with the things that we feel hold us back. But know that the Lord is interested in getting to the root of the problem and that when He deals with the core you will be able to live with much greater freedom.

30

Lead me in the way everlasting

Every year when we approach the summer I sense the same emotions from my kids. School is almost out and the thought of lying late in bed and no more homework is very enticing. Long days to relax and lounge around in your pyjamas. Evenings to stay up late and not have to do maths for 2 months sounds like heaven. What could be better?

But there's also the sense of having to leave things behind. The teacher who you have spent nearly everyday with for a whole year. The class that you have got to know. Life moves forward and that means that things change. There's a beginning and an end. Nothing ever stays the same.

Change is good for us. It adds colour to our lives and exposes us to lots of new opportunities. We get to connect with new people and try new things. It expands our horizons. When we are put into a new situation it forces us to see things differently. We are stretched and we grow. We discover new things about ourselves. Maybe we are not just as shy as we thought. May be we can learn new skills. Maybe we have more ability than we had realised.

I love creativity. I love to come up with new ideas. I love to dream with other people about what could be and to dream up a plan and make it happen. I have been involved with lots of different groups of people and have achieved lots of things. There have been times when I have thought that this is as good as it gets. I love this group of people, I love what I am doing, let's just keep things the way they are. But one thing I realise is that nothing ever lasts forever.

There have been times when I have had a great group of friends but then people have had to move away and I've felt lonely and isolated. I have felt like I am playing snakes and ladders and I've just landed on the snake and have been sent back down to the bottom of the board. Time to start over again and move slowly forward.

All of us will follow different paths in life where we will focus our time on different interests or pursuits. When I was growing up I devoted lots of years learning instruments and progressing in music. I went through grade after grade, year after year to finally complete them all. And then after all the hard work, the hours of practice and the ups and downs of trying and failing and trying again I arrived at the finish line.

You will no doubt do the same. It's very much part of life. You study, you work hard, you practise. You progress in sport, in school work, in your life skills and you move forward. When you reach each marker you have a sense of looking back and seeing your journey. You think of what it has taken to get you to where you are. The sweat and tears that no one else knows about. The fears you had before you sat the exam, The doubts you had about whether you will be able to handle your first day at your new school. That feeling that somehow everyone else seemed to be doing okay and that you were struggling.

In among all the changes and ups and down you will encounter as you journey through life there is one last thing that I want to assure you of. In simple trust each day, believe that your days are being ordered by the Lord. He goes before you into every situation to prepare blessing and favour. His way is the best way. It is a way of rest. He is always leading you into goodness. That is something that is "everlasting" His love for you will never run out. He will never not love you or work for your good. Learn to trust Him for that. That is the best way to live.

The incredible thing about your relationship with Jesus is that once it starts there is no end. Once you accept Him into your life you are connected forever. His commitment to you is not for a season. It doesn't depend on you performing well and it doesn't just grow cold over time. His love is everlasting.

As you finish this book now that this is really only the beginning of a journey. One in which you are continually uncovering the depths of His love towards you and filling your mind with the incredible truth that you are His masterpiece. We all have a choice as to what we will be mindful of. I hope that in reading this book you have found lots of truth to help you see the magnificent way that Jesus loves you. It may be that these truths are a refresher of what you have heard before or they may be new. In either case it is not about simply gathering a set of facts about God, but encountering Him and allowing Him to transform your heart and mind.

I pray that every day you would be more mindful of Jesus and His love for you, than anyone or anything else.

About the Author

Penny has been involved in ministry for over 25 years. She currently lives in Belfast where she is married with 3 great kids. With her husband she founded Exchange Church Belfast, a church family that is committed to seeing the world transformed by the grace of God. She is a certified Executive Coach and facilitator working with some of the world's biggest brands providing leadership and management development programmes. A gifted speaker and leader, Penny uses her experience as a pastor, wife & mum to connect people to the truth of God's love and grace.

You can connect with me on:

🌐 http://www.exchangechurchbelfast.com

Also by Penny Toogood

Hope Full - Thoughts to grow your confidence in the goodness of God

The world is short on hope today. Our hearts and minds are bombarded with a mixture of fear, bad news stories and dire predictions about the future.

Christian hope is more than wishing that life may change. Our hope is a strong and confident expectation of God's goodness in every area of our lives. This hope is not built on anything other than the promises of God and the gift of grace.

This devotional will help you grow in hope. Each day the truth of His word will open your heart and mind to the truth that no matter what is happening around you, you can know your best days are still to come. This is how you are called to live - Hope Full.

Available now at Amazon

Fearless - Finding Hope in uncertain times

We are living in times of unprecedented change and new challenges that are disrupting much of what we have taken for granted for so long. Uncertainty has lead many of us to experience anxiety about the future and what it may bring. The result is that fear can overshadow us and rob us of hope for tomorrow.

You do not need to live in fear. In these daily devotionals you will discover the truth that there is a better way to live. The promise of Jesus and His grace is a more powerful truth than all we face today. You will be encouraged to find new faith as you allow His word to develop fresh hope on the inside. This is how we are made to live - Fearless.

Available now at Amazon

Printed in Great Britain
by Amazon